Cuckoo

Memories from an unhappy childhood

LAWRENCE VINCENT

THE CHOIR PRESS

First published in the United Kingdom in 2019 by
The Choir Press

ISBN 978-1-78963-067-1

Introduction

In 2017 at the age of 57 I discovered that the man that I had spent my entire life thinking was my father was in fact not my biological father at all. He and my mother raised me as part of a large family of six siblings but I was a cuckoo in the nest.

Discovering this so late in life was a serious challenge to my sense of identity and triggered an avalanche of childhood memories and emotions. Therapy has taught me that this reaction was my psyche presenting evidence to my inner self that I really did exist. That even though my identity had floated free temporarily, I was real and these memories were proof of it. Over a two year period I recorded thousands of these random memories. This book contains 1,500 of them and have been included because they survived my carefully designed selection process. This process had three components. Firstly, the memories had to be from before my seventeenth birthday. This seemingly arbitrary cut-off point is important as it includes the entirety of my life spent living with my family. This is the period of my life where I was at my most disturbed, depressed and detached and provided me with my most intense memories.

My mental health improved immeasurably when I left home.

The second component was that the memories could not be free floating random thoughts but had to provoke emotions that were akin to the feelings I felt at the time.

The third component was that I had to stick to the principle of deferring to my feelings in an authentic sense and indulge the awkwardness and vulgarity that tipped out when these memories and concomitant sentiments descended on me.

It was a pleasing piece of symmetry that encouraged me to devise this selection process in the first place. My first memory in 'Cuckoo' was of watching the Charlie Chaplin film 'The Gold Rush' when he and his bearded pal are snowbound and starving and Charlie turns into a chicken in the eyes of his hallucinated partner. This vivid memory from early childhood got me thinking that I needed a process that attempted to separate genuine memories from meaningless drool and avoid the mistake of Charlie's pal.

I am in no way saying that these memories are profound or carry special meaning in the wider world. In fact the opposite is nearer to the truth as the majority are mundane in the extreme. Also, If anyone spent two years of inner solitude rummaging through the dark side of their memory bank they would also come up with a rich collection of material. I have created this book for myself to capture a bewildering set of memories that came at me from all directions in response to a traumatic event. If anybody else reads this book then I am flattered and honoured.

My parents provided me with food and shelter but on the emotional front kept me just a few degrees above the survival level. Thus there was an early unspoken challenge to me throughout my childhood to provide metaphysical grounds for wishing to exist at all. What for? And sometimes it was not fully clear to me that I did exist. Many of the memories in this book were attached to behaviours that I now know to have been provoked by a dark inner restlessness caused by my innate need to be seen and heard. As I got older I realised that like a slave labourer it was only my body that was enslaved within my family. My thoughts floated free and ensured my survival. In that sense this book is proof to myself that my childhood was real and belonged only to me.

I have unashamedly stolen the '*I remember*' format for 'Cuckoo' from Joe Brainard's iconic book of that title because the method is brilliantly simple ; to set down specific memories as they rose to the surface of consciousness and preface each refrain with '*I remember*'.

In writing 'Cuckoo' I have no ambition or interest in mythologizing the story of my life. It is simply a cathartic exercise in making sense of my early life and recording the memories that came at me when I finally learned the truth about my childhood.

Lawrence Vincent 2019

I remember watching the Charlie Chaplin film *The Gold Rush*. Charlie and his pal were so frozen and starved that his pal started thinking that Charlie was a chicken.

I remember binge reading the Billy Bunter stories in my brother's *Look and Learn* comics.

I remember a new boy starting in my infants' school and us all mobbing him when he scored a goal at playtime.

I remember the Mace delivery man dropping his box of change on our kitchen floor.

I remember silver fish on the kitchen mat.

I remember someone bringing two dead pheasants to our house.

I remember feeling jealous of anyone living in a new house.

I remember saving up the coupons from Robertson's jam labels and sending off for a pot gollywog. It was the first parcel I ever received.

I remember regretting that I hadn't chosen the gollywog badge instead.

I remember dreading my paper round on Fridays as I had extra papers to deliver.

I remember creating a snooker game using marbles, tent poles and an empty Andrew's Liver Salts tin.

I remember hating my sister cutting my hair as the fringe was always wonky.

I remember having a strong impulse to throw my father's shaving mug through the kitchen window.

I remember my father telling me off for spitting and me claiming that it wasn't me it was cuckoo spit.

I remember having a recurrent dream that I was a bird trapped in the corner of my bedroom.

I remember being terrified of Mrs Marshall's adult down syndrome son.

I remember being taken to the railway signalman's box by Mr. Vause and making toasted jam sandwiches on the open fire.

I remember leaving school without having a single conversation with my parents about what I was going to do next.

I remember changing the labels on the hot and cold bath taps and my brother going crazy because I wouldn't tell him how I did it.

I remember my mother having a total meltdown every Christmas Eve.

I remember my friend Stuart dying in a motorbike accident and the look on his dad's face at his funeral.

I remember a David Cassidy poster.

I remember seeing big tufts of Mrs Blackburn's pubic hair as she bent down in front of me to pick peas.

I remember my sister stashing stuff away for her 'bottom drawer' (I had no idea what that was).

I remember eating luncheon meat for tea every Sunday.

I remember my sister eating a huge bowlful of strawberries and denying it (she still does).

I remember my parents not coming home one night and Nellie Wardle calling looking for her husband Jim.

I remember wearing a tea cosy as a hat.

I remember going into the village after I came home from hospital and the big kids calling me Jesus because everyone thought I had died.

I remember cooking Yorkshire puddings in the coal fire oven.

I remember Don Betts wandering towards an oncoming train at South Milford station.

I remember seeing a huge eel in the beck.

I remember apple fights in Farah's derelict house.

I remember the first Ford Capris.

I remember my friend Tosh going to stay with his mother for the summer and coming back with the word 'cheers' for thank you.

I remember lying that I had felt a girl's breasts.

I remember my first cigarette and how much it made me spit.

I remember winning loads of money at 3 card brag and skipping school to buy a new pair of Levi's from the Army and Navy store in Selby.

I remember walking home from the air show and being so hungry that someone gave me a sugar sandwich.

I remember bags of dried peas on the pantry shelf. They had a weird lump in them (salt?).

I remember my mother telling my father that he looked nice in a clean newly ironed white shirt.

I remember my headmaster Mr. Burnley scratching his head and doing a weird dance movement with his fingers.

I remember falling off a rope swing and crashing into the beck.

I remember building an underground den and my brother destroying it because he said it wasn't safe.

I remember my brother wearing clogs that he had brought back from Sweden and my mates teasing me about it.

I remember the furry dice in my sister's boyfriend's car.

I remember never seeing our neighbour Dr. Mcandlish.

I remember somebody in the village having his leg cut off because he smoked non-tipped cigarettes.

I remember Ken Hill the butcher's dad taking ten pence pieces out of the till and stuffing them in his pocket when he thought I wasn't looking (I was in the shop buying potted meat).

I remember my form teacher on the first day of secondary school telling Jane Sowden to wash her make up off. She flatly refused and after that I had the most intense sexual fantasies about her. I never acted on them as she only went out with much older boys.

I remember Broggy Pawson.

I remember thinking that all weathermen were called Jack Frost.

I remember carol singing outside a pub. We were brought inside and stood on a table to sing. We made a fortune.

I remember the smell of burning pumpkin lanterns.

I remember hating the sensation of having sticky lips after eating candy floss.

I remember how silent everything was on Sundays.

I remember starting to collect stamps and then packing it in really quickly.

I remember trying really hard not to do anything that could be interpreted as queer.

I remember green boxes of fruit gums. They were shaped like fruits unlike the ones in tubes.

I remember my friend Tosh telling me I could have one of his cigarettes if I told him what the hardest part of the human body was. Phil Varley was behind him secretly giving me the answer by pointing to his teeth. He wasn't being altruistic, he claimed half of the cigarette.

I remember claiming that I had left a book at school, so I could avoid walking past a kid I was scared of.

I remember Mick Ransome could catch flies in his hand.

I remember getting stung by a bee and my father sucking out the poison and spitting.

I remember laughing in church at Mrs. Pawson's warbly voice.

I remember the best part of school dinners was the ice-cold water in the metal jugs.

I remember knowing that it wasn't normal to hate going home.

I remember thinking that Simon Langrick's dad was an alcoholic.

I remember not always going to the toilet when I needed a pee.

I remember the music from the Edgar Wallace mysteries.

I remember my father's 'world famous soup' every Boxing Day.

I remember wondering if all black people were poor.

I remember seeing the sea for the first time.

I remember never having the confidence to tell a long joke.

I remember thinking it was absurd that I was studying Geoffrey Chaucer.

I remember my father putting a load of Brylcreem in my hair on the morning of my sister's wedding.

I remember the 'nigger' money box.

I remember not turning up for a date with Lynette Milner and saying it was because I had spent all my money on flowers for my friend's grave (I was lying).

I remember having sexual fantasies about both Sutcliffe twins.

I remember my brother getting a holiday job as a dustman.

I remember going to Martin Holroyd's house and seeing a pair of Y fronts with a black swastika on them.

I remember being squirted with brown sauce.

I remember a new bench and that somebody carved their initials into it before it had been there a full day.

I remember shuffling knee deep in piles of fallen leaves.

I remember being afraid of small things but brave about big things.

I remember playing football with a running commentary going on in my head like I was a world-famous player.

I remember my father telling me that you can tell how a person votes by the newspaper they read. He asked me to tell him who gets which paper. He was shocked when I told him that I delivered the *Morning Star* to number 98 High Street.

I remember my Father telling me that the people at number 98 must be communists. I peered through their living room window the next morning and there actually was a poster of Che Guevara on the living room wall. I told my father and he said 'ye gods'.

I remember Chinese burns.

I remember playing Pudsey juniors at football and losing 26-0.

I remember my father losing a bet with Derek Robinson when Castleford beat Salford in the Rugby League Challenge Cup Final.

I remember the man who worked in the garage had a German wife called Erica.

I remember my grandma liked to watch wrestling on a Saturday afternoon and how contemptuous my father was about it.

I remember my father telling me that a truck that drove past with 'Campbell and Penty' on the side used be 'Campbell Penty and Vincent'.

I remember the iron barrier at the end of back lane.

I remember pressing wild flowers between sheets of newspaper.

I remember my father doing a decorating job for someone and they refused to pay him. It was the first time I heard him say 'bastard'.

I remember the plank you walked over to get across the beck.

I remember being scared of barbed wire.

I remember eating pear windfalls from Arthur Cawood's lawn when I delivered his *Farmer's Weekly* magazine.

I remember not being able to stop putting my tongue on the electrodes of a battery.

I remember mincemeat spewing out of a mincing machine.

I remember the shiny copper bottom of the marmalade pan.

I remember eating a whole pan full of chips and my mother telling me I will be constipated.

I remember the red handkerchief poking out of the pocket of my father's suede jacket.

I remember my mother making a hat and how mortified I was when she wore it to the school parents' evening.

I remember watching the FA Cup final at Reg Harker's house.

I remember using the outdoor toilet at the Black Bull pub and seeing a man buying condoms. He had a cigarette sticking out of his mouth as he put his money into the machine.

I remember going to the Great Yorkshire Show.

I remember breaking into Steeton Hall to find the ghosts.

I remember my father coming to find me in the village to tell me not to go home or I would get a beating from my mother for not making my bed. *I remember* thinking he was a cowardly cunt. I stayed out until hunger drove me home.

I remember my eldest sister pouring neat vinegar on one of my other sister's heat spots and her screaming.

I remember my sisters dressing up my younger brother, painting his nails and calling him 'Pepe'.

I remember stealing detonators from a hut on the railway. I was planning to blow up my mother whilst she slept but Phil Varley's dad saw that I had them and took them off me.

I remember seeing my friend Tosh's back after his father had beaten him with a cane.

I remember spending the first two weeks of secondary school in a pair of non-uniform trousers because my parents didn't get me the right ones. I was bullied by staff and kids because of it. It meant I had to fight other kids and therefore get a bad reputation which stayed with me for the following five years.

I remember stealing a ten pence piece from Michael Finan's bedroom and his mother asking me about it when I next went round his house.

I remember shitting my trunks on holiday. I went to the public toilets to try and clean myself up but I left the door of the cubicle unlocked. Somebody walked in and everybody saw me caked in shit.

I remember my older brother being bullied at school and stealing the PE shoe of his bully and burning it in our garden.

I remember being hung upside down over a bridge by two of my brother's friends.

I remember my younger brother being born and somebody visiting and leaving a small teddy bear on his pram.

I remember somebody stealing the stuffed robin from the nativity scene in the doctor's surgery and being scared that people would think it was me.

I remember stealing a pretend bar of chocolate from infants school. I stuffed it down my trousers and was terrified all day.

I remember squeezing David Kirk's ear lobe in the mouth of my toy crocodile.

I remember auditioning for the school choir with Mrs Tate. She told me I couldn't join and I did that terrible trying to hold my tears in thing.

I remember using all my paper round money to buy my mother bath salts for her birthday and she shouted at me because they made her vagina sting.

I remember being made to eat a suet dumpling that hadn't been cooked properly.

I remember devoting a whole day to thinking of creative ways to kill my mother.

I remember feeling jealous because I saw my father give my sister three half crowns for her riding lesson and he never gave me money.

I remember always eating porridge with Carnation milk.

I remember always feeling unsafe on holiday as we were abandoned all day whilst my parents went drinking.

I remember an older boy taking me into the derelict house in the village and masturbating in front of me.

I remember my mother battering me in front of my father and instead of stopping her he told her to avoid hitting me on my head.

I remember blocking up the toilet with loo paper. I was so scared I stuffed all the paper out of the bathroom window. When I went outside it was all hanging off the holly tree.

I remember being constipated and straining so hard I thought my head might explode.

I remember my brother's friend locking me in the shed and making me hit his erect penis with a toffee hammer.

I remember being put into bed for a daytime nap next to my father who was sleeping off the night shift.

I remember random red poppies in corn fields.

I remember eating liver and thinking it tasted of piss.

I remember us kids fighting over who got the wishbone from the Christmas turkey. It was my turn one year and *I remember* wishing that nobody would get polio.

I remember my father telling me that when miners get rehoused from slums to new council housing that they keep their coal in the bath.

I remember individually wrapped Wilkinson Sword razor blades.

I remember an argument about Nimble bread.

I remember noticing that Peter Lorimer had an erection whilst he was lining up for the national anthems before a World Cup match.

I remember thinking that Johan Cruyff was super cool for giving his press conferences in different languages.

I remember thinking that Johan Cruff was very good looking and wondering if I was homosexual.

I remember how thin the paper was in school bibles.

I remember Mr. Rutherford giving me toffees from a brightly coloured tin.

I remember sneezing eleven times.

I remember seeing a Manchester United fan outside Elland Road with a big streak of green snot down the sleeve of his Crombie.

I remember an older kid called Skippy getting his hair permed.

I remember Andrew Sands always rode his bike by using his toes on the pedals rather than his whole foot.

I remember cheap coal was called slack.

I remember someone blowing himself up by sawing through an empty gas bottle.

I remember a whole row of new shiny dustbins with black rubber lids.

I remember eating raw peas and seeing them in my turd the next day.

I remember always having to count stuff.

I remember playing table tennis with a dented ball.

I remember the sexy photograph of Christine Keeler.

I remember finding the Dorian Grey story creepy.

I remember feeling like I had never wiped my arse properly.

I remember some coal miners getting trapped down a mine shaft.

I remember never being able to float on my back in the pool. I always panicked and flipped myself over.

I remember stripey HB pencils.

I remember that when one kid wanted to go to the toilet in infants school the whole class wanted to go.

I remember a strange floaty feeling when I closed my eyes on a sunny day.

I remember designing new paper planes and my teacher letting me go outside to test them.

I remember that no matter how sad I felt in the evening I always felt better the next morning.

I remember walking through a cornfield drunk.

I remember how delicious it felt to get into bed when exhausted.

I remember asking girls to meet me after school. They would often agree but I would bottle out and have to take huge detours to avoid them.

I remember always lying when asked to say anything about my family in school (for example 'what did you do over the summer').

I remember talking to Philip Wilkinson about Debbie Gannon's huge breasts. He said that he knew for sure that she stuffed hankies down her bra. I asked him how he knew and he did that tapping his nose thing.

I remember my teacher saying that balsa wood is soft wood when in fact it is hard wood.

I remember never having enough pairs of underpants.

I remember kipper ties.

I remember wondering how people wear 'car coats' when I always feel so hot and sick in a car.

I remember my mother going into hospital. We got a home help called Mrs Midgely and my mother bitched her out from her hospital bed for ironing our underwear.

I remember staring into a mirror for so long that I got a weird detached feeling and I became a stranger.

I remember women from the new estate blocking the bus route.

I remember my mother cleaning my ears with a match.

I remember always having to get into my brother's second hand bath water.

I remember the giant compass Mr. Burnley used to use on the blackboard.

I remember drawing a picture of Winston Churchill and my teacher saying it looked more like the fat one in Laurel and Hardy.

I remember a black student teacher at my secondary school and somebody calling her a 'chocolate drop'.

I remember sweet cigarettes and how the odd one didn't have a red tip.

I remember getting drunk on sherry. Afterwards I thought it was something homosexuals probably did and that it must not happen again.

I remember not having a TV but pretending we had a colour TV.

I remember never bringing friends home.

I remember seeing a frog in the back yard grate.

I remember kicking a football against the back wall of the coal shed and trying to shut the door before it bounced out. If I didn't do it five times in a row I thought something bad was going to happen.

I remember my dad would always eat bread and butter with his tinned peaches.

I remember our neighbour's bald head.

I remember my mother painting freckles on her nose because she wanted to look like Twiggy.

I remember Uncle Percy coming to our house and my father making me promise not to tell mother.

I remember my aunt visiting from Sweden and bringing a big box of ginger biscuits.

I remember the excruciating pain of the penicillin needle going into my legs when I was in hospital.

I remember the IRA blowing up Lord Mountbatten.

I remember that the first man I ever saw with tattoos was Charlie Bray.

I remember my father was always rude about Leeds but nice about York.

I remember always wanting to be gambling.

I remember feeling scared of Chairman Mao.

I remember 'Light up the sky with Standard fireworks'

I remember feeling repulsed by the seeds clustered together inside a melon (I still get this reaction).

I remember girls playing hopscotch while boys played football in the school yard.

I remember 'Kingston House'.

I remember the sound of the vacuum cleaner made me feel calm (still does).

I remember always having a great Christmas tree.

I remember getting 'Biggles' books from the mobile library.

I remember a drunk woman pissing whilst standing up outside our house.

I remember out telephone number changing from 436 to 2436.

I remember my mother refusing to cut back the hollyhocks in the front garden. She was told to do so because they were restricting the vision of motorists pulling out of the junction next to our house. Somebody cut them down one night and the story got into the local newspaper.

I remember how dark it was in Lunn's cycle repair shop.

I remember my younger sister used to rub herself against furniture. We called it 'the dirty trick'.

I remember my first Wimpy burger.

I remember watching 'Top of the Pops' and knowing it represented something bigger and more exciting than my life.

I remember my father trying to turn the stereo off at the socket with his shoes on and smashing the plug.

I remember 'Shin' Green's broad bean poles poking over the top of his garden wall.

I remember Mr. Burnley's tie pin.

I remember packets of crisps containing tiny bags of salt.

I remember my mother losing her temper with me and telling me that if I ever go back into hospital she won't visit me.

I remember my father coming home from a night shift and waking me up to watch a live World Cup football match with him.

I remember walking through a wet field in a pair of new blue trainers and all the dye coming off on my feet.

I remember being jealous of boys with long hair.

I remember being chased across the cricket field by a dog called Henry.

I remember my infants school teacher cooking food for kids she discovered had been sent to school without breakfast. I pretended to be one of them to get egg on toast.

I remember asking for scraps with a bag of chips and the woman serving gave me a secret fish. She put her finger to her lips to tell me it was our secret.

I remember Paul Newman eating fifty hard boiled eggs in the film *'Cool Hand Luke'*. I tried to get my friends to bet against me doing it. They didn't because we couldn't raise enough money to buy the eggs.

I remember the huge oak tree in the corner of the cricket field.

I remember 'Cat Ballou'.

I remember putting chewing gum on a stick and poking it through the gaps in the floor boards of the cricket pavilion to snag the loose change that had fallen down there.

I remember a woman telling me I had beautiful eyes.

I remember sycamore windmills.

I remember the A and B buttons in public telephone boxes.

I remember not being able to run in cricket pads.

I remember playing football on my own on the front lawn and somebody shouting 'hey Georgie Best' from a passing car.

I remember knitting needles with little numbers on them.

I remember a weird boggle eyed rabbit with a disease that I couldn't pronounce the name of.

I remember Pete and Andy's mobile disco. They wore really crap denim waistcoats with Pete and Andy's mobile discos embroided on the back of them.

I remember a giant bagatelle board.

I remember the bar billiards table in the Ash Tree pub.

I remember Chris Muggeridge's girlfriend putting on loads of weight. He said it was because she was on the pill.

I remember kicking a muddy football against a clean white sheet that was hanging on the clothes line.

I remember a rumour that Gerald Yeoman's brother had sex with his dog.

I remember my father telling me that my grandfather had a fat stomach because he carried heavy mortar shells in a belt in the first world war and it destroyed his stomach muscles.

I remember an old humming top.

I remember the Avon Cosmetics factory.

I remember my father cycling to Leeds to save money on the train fare and getting his bicycle stolen.

I remember shitting in the bath and pretending the turd was a submarine.

I remember finding out that Tosh got paid to be in the church choir. I then tried to join and the Vicar told me that it was wrong to be motivated by money.

I remember doing a school project where we went to interview the Methodist minister Mr. Chapman. He invited us to sit at the kitchen table and he cleared the crumbs on the table cloth with his hands.

I remember my brother collecting birds' eggs.

I remember the three day week.

I remember my mother saying that the actor Alan Ladd was so small that he had to stand on a box to kiss his leading ladies.

I remember Steve Benton's mother winning £7,000 on *Spot the Ball.*

I remember Lester Hill giving me a highland toffee chew.

I remember my father telling me that in the pub mild is cheaper than bitter.

I remember the smell of tins of Lakeland pencils.

I remember Jane Sowden cheating at a spelling test.

I remember the sand martin nests on the side of the building merchant.

I remember an older boy in my village, Gerald Addison dying. My youth club created a table tennis tournament in his honour.

I remember the Spaghetti House siege.

I remember hyper inflation in Argentina.

I remember a teacher telling me I had a terrible reputation.

I remember doing a school project on ancient Egypt.

I remember the sweat dripping off a man who was hammering a post into the ground at the village sports day.

I remember a mobile fruit and vegetable shop.

I remember picking out the seeds from a pomegranate individually with a pin.

I remember everything plastic seemed to be made in Hong Kong.

I remember Carlos the Jackal.

I remember pressing the refund button in a public telephone box and money dropping out.

I remember a shooting stick.

I remember opening the back door on a windy day when the front door was open. It slammed and smashed.

I remember putting the spokes into a penny farthing bike.

I remember sauternes wine at Christmas.

I remember home made madeira cake.

I remember skimming stones.

I remember cricket teas.

I remember breaking into the school tuck shop.

I remember the boating lake in Pontefract park.

I remember my friend tosh playing football with a box of matches in his pocket. He fell on them and they burst into flames and burned his leg.

I remember that Mick Ransome was an uncle to a nephew who was older than him. It confused us all.

I remember finding a polaroid photograph in the street of a man in a car holding his penis.

I remember a girl with learning difficulties using the baby swings at the park.

I remember the Dave Allen show. He always smoked cigarettes and drank whiskey whilst telling his jokes.

I remember a rumour that a girl in school was made pregnant by her own father.

I remember the dandruff on Mr. Minards' shoulders.

I remember the Munich Olympic massacre.

I remember my father making me feel afraid of Russia.

I remember Ken Hull wearing a pair of Chelsea football shorts.

I remember the cooling towers falling down at Ferrybridge power station and killing a load of men.

I remember collecting my Saturday evening paper round from Miss. Jackson's house and the smell of freshly baked bread.

I remember my grandfather's grave did not have a headstone and we weren't allowed to talk about it.

I remember piles of sugar beet.

I remember Charlie George's cup final winning goal for Arsenal and the way he lay on the floor after he scored it.

I remember 'The Prisoner'.

I remember an Australian cricketer called Keith Stackpole.

I remember thinking that Johnny Thornton was very good looking.

I remember the fat actor in Z Cars was called Stratford Johns.

I remember the foul smell in the bottom of the tooth brush mug.

I remember my father not inhaling when he smoked an occasional cigarette (he was a pipe smoker).

I remember seeing an old photograph of my grandmother and thinking that she looked like an Inca.

I remember an old woman in the village had a beard.

I remember the boy next door had a plaster on one of his glasses lenses because he had a lazy eye.

I remember Rosemary Poundford dancing on the TV show 'Junior Showtime'.

I remember arguing with the youth worker because I wanted to play the whole 'Deep Purple in Rock" LP and the girls complained.

I remember reading about trench foot and then trying to get it by walking for ages in the beck.

I remember my father saying that if Cassius Clay had been white he never would have been stripped of his world title for refusing the Vietnam draft.

I remember a boy eating a worm.

I remember wondering what The Queen does every day.

I remember the Moors Murderers.

I remember writing a girl's phone number on a bit of paper and losing it. I found it months later in the willow pattern cup in the top left hand of the welsh dresser. Her name was Valerie Steele.

I remember hearing about a huge hail stone that had a fish in it.

I remember Mick Finan flying to Spain. He was the first person in the village to go abroad.

I remember Arthur Ashe winning Wimbledon.

I remember something about France and Algeria on the news.

I remember the first time I went to the cinema. I saw 'Towering Inferno'.

I remember losing my return train ticket. I borrowed money from my mates to get home and then found it in my match box.

I remember Anne Rowe putting her hand down my trousers. It felt really weird and I thought there must be something wrong with me.

I remember perfecting a brilliant serve at table tennis.

I remember the joy of an ice cold glass of water after working up that intense thirst that only kids get.

I remember Geoff Thornton's father chain smoking Capstan full strength cigarettes.

I remember a man from the new estate giving me money to settle his newspaper bill when I delivered his paper. I wasn't supposed to take money off customers but I did and kept it.

I remember that Barry Ward never wore a shirt. He only ever wore vests.

I remember when cheese cloth shirts were the height of fashion.

I remember knowing it was weird that my mother was always prancing around in front of us naked.

I remember my brother over using the word 'suave'.

I remember feeling sad when I heard Christmas carols.

I remember Graham Hill's mother boiling pants in a big pot on the stove.

I remember when the Oldfield twins started school they had their own language.

I remember watching girls play a weird gymnastics type game with elastic.

I remember how embarrassed I was by the string of plastic fruit that hung in our kitchen.

I remember watching *Dr. Finlay's Casebook* on Sunday evening.

I remember Graham Hill's father drowning a litter of kittens in a sack.

I remember always holding in my tears.

I remember growing a single crocus in a yoghurt pot.

I remember a famine in Biafra.

I remember using a machine that dispensed fresh eggs called the 'Automatic Hen'.

I remember *Readers Digest* sending a big book on wild animals. I hid it as I knew my father would send it back. I loved that book and kept it hidden for years.

I remember my older brother doing really rubbish Monty Python impersonations.

I remember day dreams of moving to a big city and living alone.

I remember a kid much younger than me dropping a half crown piece on the grass at the church fete. I snaffled it before he could find it and blew it on the tombola stall. I won a red plastic solitaire set.

I remember once waking up outside and the first thing I saw was a goose.

I remember finding a big sack of toys in our attic. I was so excited as it was just before Christmas and I assumed they were for us kids. They never materialised though and I still wonder who they were for.

I remember going to the Yorkshire Show and not knowing it cost to get in. I blew all my money on the admission charge and spent all day anxious about food.

I remember sometimes getting please and thank you mixed up.

I remember trying to make my new school bag look old.

I remember the PG Tips tea advert where monkeys were moving a piano.

I remember never believing in the things I was supposed to believe in like God and Santa Claus and the tooth fairy.

I remember the sawdust on the floor of the butcher's shop.

I remember once working out exactly how many seconds it was before I broke up for the summer holidays. It was in May so it was quite a calculation.

I remember the panic when somebody sent a Christmas card to my parents who they hadn't sent one to.

I remember a dark red matt Christmas tree bauble.

I remember potted meat wrapped very neatly in wax paper.

I remember how skinny and blonde David Capper was.

I remember always thinking that when kids didn't have dads it was because they were in jail for robbing banks.

I remember the first thing I ever wore round my neck was a St. Christopher on a silver chain. It got ripped off during a fight and I couldn't repair it so I dropped it down a grate.

I remember finding the Salvation Army creepy.

I remember always thinking that bad men like Al Capone and Ronnie Biggs were cool.

I remember being obsessed with changing how things looked my closing one eye.

I remember a game show on TV where the contestant had to eat a giant potato to win the prize. The contestant got to choose how it was cooked. He chose mashed and failed. My mother said he should have chosen chips as they would slide down more easily.

I remember buying a pen knife and spending hours whittling sticks.

I remember the football changing room in the village was an old gypsy wagon.

I remember loving marbles (I still do).

I remember big slabs of pink and white nougat in a shop window.

I remember my mother was always rude about other women.

I remember the fair coming to Sherburn and how going always felt edgy and dangerous.

I remember cracking the 12 times table before the 9s.

I remember putting a note on my bedroom door telling people to keep out. I was showing off because I had just learned to write.

I remember never taking a crap in a public toilet.

I remember always getting bored before the end of Monopoly.

I remember my Headmaster Mr Burnley's crisp blue summer shirt. He wore it outside his trousers and without a tie like a Colonel in a hot country.

I remember Mick Finan's parents (Doreen and Colin) used to call each other Gina (Lollobrigida) and Rock (Hudson).

I remember hearing that Errol Flynn had a huge penis that had to be strapped to his leg in case it got frisky during his sexy scenes.

I remember a window full of saucy postcards in Bridlington.

I remember David Kirk going to see Pele play at Hillsborough. We didn't believe he had seen the great man so he brought the programme to school to prove it.

I remember a gay bar in Leeds called 'the Griffin'.

I remember a national front pub in Leeds called the 'Scarboro Taps'.

I remember my older brother had a stars and stripes vest.

I remember trying to memorise random stuff for no good reason.

I remember the first live band I ever saw was "The Sensational Alex Harvey Band" at Leeds University.

I remember stealing money from my father and buying loads of sweets with it. I framed my sister by planting the wrappers in the bin in her bedroom. It worked.

I remember my friend's sister getting killed. She got out of a car and her long scarf got trapped in the door. The car drove off and strangled her.

I remember going to David Uttley's house. His father was the village policeman and he was frying bacon in his uniform.

I remember my brother's toy blue boat with 'Staithes' written on it.

I remember the milkman was always nice to me when I was doing my paper round. It felt like we were early morning comrades in a sleeping world.

I remember going to Maskell's barbers for a 'short back and sides and plenty off the top'.

I remember Mr.Vause's front lawn was a putting green and one day he let me have a go.

I remember seeing a man's knobbly hands and my father saying it was because of arthritis.

I remember the 'Spike' in the kitchen cupboard that my father used for important paperwork.

I remember the oil smell on my father's work clothes.

I remember playing Subbuteo for hours on the dining room table.

I remember my brother going to Cornwall on a camping holiday.

I remember the fear I felt when hearing my mother coming down the stairs.

I remember pressed tongue at Christmas.

I remember us getting a new Grundig stereo.

I remember the Peter Stuyvesant adverts on *Radio Caroline'*.

I remember being given pea soup at my friend's house. I hated it and my friend told me I had to eat it or his mother would be cross.

I remember building a tree house in the common lane woods.

I remember feeling ashamed of my father whenever he cycled past me and my friends.

I remember working out that musical taste was a tribal (class?) thing. Posh kids liked *Yes* and *Genesis* and kids like me liked *Led Zeppelin* and *Deep Purple*.

I remember joining a band at school. We were going to perform the Peter Frampton song 'Show me the Way' in school assembly. I bottled out and regretted it when I saw the attention my replacement got from girls.

I remember wanting a Kaftan coat and never getting one.

I remember always having to save up for stuff and never getting anything bought for me.

I remember thinking the leaves on a pansy plant were like little velvet cushions.

I remember the smell of fresh putty.

I remember Edwin Courts designing a system of string in his bedroom that turned on the radio when the door was opened.

I remember the nice smell of the powder the barber put on the back of my neck.

I remember a big penny money box (1966) on the piano. The stopper at the bottom was lost so it was useless.

I remember a boat trip on the river at Ruswarp.

I remember literally pouring sweat out of my trainers.

I remember Caramac bars tasted sweeter than other chocolate.

I remember a weird hand sign that kids used to do to symbolise sexual intercourse.

I remember the strange red logo in the right hand corner of the Daily Express.

I remember thinking that nobody would ever call their son Adolf (my theory was fine until my first year of teaching in London when I had an Adolf and a Hermann in my English class. My impulse was to keep them apart!).

I remember lots of hair clips.

I remember waiting my turn in the corner shop and Mr. Maskell in front of me asked for a pot of mustard. The shopkeeper asked him if he wanted English or French. He said he wanted Coleman's.

I remember the way the barber used to snip the air with his scissors.

I remember how contemptuous my father was on anyone who threw turkey away at Christmas.

I remember thinking that everything about my family was shameful and embarrassing.

I remember my mother always wore a housecoat and hardly ever got dressed.

I remember my mother putting Bell's whiskey in her tea.

I remember my father's shiny red pyjamas.

I remember the smell of Pond's face cream.

I remember shaking a tambourine in the school assembly.

I remember thinking that I belonged somewhere else.

I remember parkin on bonfire night.

I remember my younger sister used to put so much hairspray in her hair that it went totally stiff.

I remember eating cake mix from the bowl.

I remember watching a film and being intrigued by the beauty spot on the face of the actress. I think it was Moonfleet.

I remember getting a new bike and it was already too small for me.

I remember my sister spending all her money on the first day of a family holiday.

I remember my father shouting at my mother when he discovered how much she had spent with Kay's catalogue.

I remember always wanting ice cream.

I remember getting fish and chips on holiday. I asked why I couldn't have a big fish and my mother started crying.

I remember some adults joining our football game.
One of them said I was useless.

I remember having an argument with someone who
said money always makes you happy.

I remember hand-me-down jumpers.

I remember the smell of floor polish.

I remember the anchor tattoo on Barry Ward's arm.

I remember somebody from my village setting off for
Timbuktu and getting as far as Yugoslavia.

I remember Mrs Crowe giving me barley sugar sweets
to help with travel sickness.

I remember asking Dulcie Close what the word
trespass meant on a sign.

I remember my father accosting David Varey as he had
been hassling my sister.

I remember Vesta chow mein ready meals.

I remember tasting yoghurt for the first time.

I remember not being allowed to go swimming with
the school because I always puked on the coach.

I remember my father's woolly swimming trunks.

I remember parcels from Kay's catalogue.

I remember creating a fake four leaf clover.

I remember being exhausted and trying to stay awake.

I remember having ten teeth extracted in one go and waking up and puking blood.

I remember the sound of the church organ.

I remember Sunday night baths and dreading the hair wash.

I remember a boy in hospital with crushed legs.

I remember learning how to play knock out whist.

I remember finding some old church posters with my grandad's name on them in the bottom of a cupboard.

I remember my father grew sweet peas on the broad bean poles.

I remember the sound the garage door made when it scraped across the ground.

I remember trying to find out what 'lumpen proletariat' meant in the Pear's junior encyclopaedia but not knowing where to look.

I remember my sister stepping on some glass. Her big toe kept bleeding even though she put on loads of plasters. She probably should have gone to the hospital, but nobody took her.

I remember thinking that the smell of sileage was even worse than manure.

I remember not knowing what 'kerb your dog' meant.

I remember the overpowering smell of tomatoes in the greenhouse.

I remember lining up caterpillars on the windowsill.

I remember hearing about wet dreams and wondering why I never had them.

I remember a girl giving herself love bites by squeezing her flesh with the top from a fairly liquid bottle.

I remember how hyper aware everyone was in school of the toughness pecking order.

I remember Olympic sized swimming pools and not really knowing how they were different to normal swimming pools.

I remember a school trip to Hull docks and seeing men working bare chested even though it was really cold.

I remember the tiny boxes on football coupons.

I remember often trying to work out if I felt bad about something bad I had done or whether I felt bad for not feeling bad.

I remember all the teachers hating Ian Henshaw except the drama teacher who loved him because he could do back flips from a standing start.

I remember feeling what a crap deal it was getting a second-hand bath. You get the dirty water and have to clean the bath. It seemed like seriously rough justice to me.

I remember putting neat bleach on my jeans and regretting it as it burned holes in them.

I remember thinking all read and black butterflies were Red Admirals.

I remember the unbearably loud noise a Vulcan jet made at the Church Fenton air show.

I remember an argument about what made the best weapon; a catapult or a bow and arrow.

I remember Keith Richards couldn't work out if he wanted to be Keith Richards or Keith Richard.

I remember my father telling me I was like my mother's father. It really upset me as I knew he didn't like him.

I remember chocolate snowballs and how we would try and eat the cream inside and leave the chocolate shell to last.

I remember my older sister was always sketching designs for new clothes.

I remember small packets of chewing gum with five pieces in them.

I remember a pair of flared check trousers that I seemed to wear for years.

I remember a man in the village who stopped on his bike on the main road because he saw his wife and new baby coming towards him. A truck killed him and it all happened in front of her.

I remember the string of spit that came out of my father's mouth when he took out his false teeth.

I remember a small pot with matches in it. The outside of the pot was coated in sandpaper.

I remember thinking how unfair it was that I had to earn all my money when other kids got given loads from their parents.

I remember leather sandals with little holes in them shaped like the spades in a deck of playing cards.

I remember getting presents at Christmas that didn't feel like real Christmas presents, like a coat.

I remember Miss Wright hitting my hand with a ruler and getting angry because I wouldn't show that it hurt.

I remember feeling that the only thing in my life that was lucky was that my birthday was in the school holidays and I avoided a ducking.

I remember not being able to work out how kids get to join organisations like the scouts.

I remember turning bus tickets into school dinner tickets. I felt like the master forger from a war film.

I remember 'He's a poet but he doesn't know it'.

I remember my father using the word 'Wog' as a general term of abuse regardless of someone's ethnicity.

I remember running into the Chinese takeaway and shouting 'hello my old china' (an old Yorkshire saying) for a bet.

I remember a dog that was so old and fat its stomach dragged on the ground.

I remember that Billy Bunter went to Greyfriars School.

I remember how badly dubbed the *Three White Horses* TV show was.

I remember smoking weed with Michael Ryan.

I remember an *Ink Spots* 78 r.p.m. record in the attic.

I remember playing tennis when stoned with half a tennis ball.

I remember burning my mouth really badly on a battered potato fritter from the chip shop.

I remember wondering what the point of paint by numbers was.

I remember Zorro.

I remember my father always thought that people who go to see the doctor are trying to skive off work.

I remember cutting open a bull's eye.

I remember Elizabeth Taylor and Richard Burton kept getting married.

I remember Mick Jones skinning Bob Mcnab down the right wing and crossing the ball to Alan Clarke. He was stood on the penalty spot and sent a perfect header into the bottom right hand corner of the the goal. I was so happy.

I remember 'Richard of York gave battle in vain' was the method of remembering the colours of the rainbow.

I remember watching two men have a really violent fight outside the 'Threepenny Bit' pub in Leeds.

I remember sheets of toy transfers.

I remember black jacks.

I remember accidentally mincing up a frog with the lawn mower.

I remember starting domino games with double six.

I remember the inside of my nose drying out and how painful and crispy it was.

I remember the Norman Hunter, Frannie Lee fight. Norman Hunter won of course.

I remember someone stealing the lead off the church roof (it wasn't me!).

I remember my father taking marmalade sandwiches to work.

I remember my father telling me his hip flask was made of pewter.

I remember drawing a lion and it was put up on the classroom wall.

I remember trying to join the fire brigade and being told I was too skinny.

I remember learning to play patience.

I remember pretending to put a shilling in the church collection plate but really stealing half a crown.

I remember a pile of criss cross candle wax on the mantle piece.

I remember the row of slum houses in Micklefield called 'Sunny bank'.

I remember a cookery show called 'The Galloping Gourmet'. He used to grab a woman from the audience to eat with him and there would be much shrieking and excitement. I found it really annoying.

I remember the Flower Pot Men (who doesn't?).

I remember the juke box in the milk bar in Sherburn.

I remember the Avon lady coming to the house.

I remember Mr. Burnley telling us that when he was in India with the army it was so hot it was possible to fry eggs on the pavement.

I remember a book by Edmund Hillary.

I remember giving Sandra Culkin a plastic ring that I got from a lucky bag. I was so appalled that I had done it that I avoided her for the rest of my childhood. She must have thought I was very fickle.

I remember not knowing if Jimmy Clitheroe was a man or a boy.

I remember asking my granddad why the Germans in a war film were talking English.

I remember seeing a York City scarf in my friend's house and trying to figure out a way to steal it.

I remember a friend of my sister staying over and seeing her in her underwear.

I remember snuff.

I remember hearing that my Auntie Valerie had married a bigamist.

I remember my mother complaining that the Sunday roast beef was tough.

I remember Neil Fisher and Gavin Borrowdale wearing identical Addidas trainers.

I remember mispronouncing evaporated. I said it like ever-ported and everyone laughed.

I remember Pickering's pie filling.

I remember Milk of Magnesia.

I remember my brother smoking Chesterfield cigarettes.

I remember learning to strike a match in that really cool way when you leave it in the match book.

I remember smashing the coconut I won at the fair with an axe.

I remember getting my fingers trapped in the door of a Ford Humber.

I remember loving alcohol so much that I knew it would become a problem for me later (it did).

I remember telling Brian Woodhouse that his girlfriend was ugly and feeling bad about it for ages afterwards.

I remember getting winded in a fight and a stranger bending me over to help me get my breath back.

I remember wanting to go to America.

I remember walking to Sherburn library to read about heroin.

I remember getting my desert boots stitched up at the cobblers and realising it was a waste of money as they became too narrow to wear.

I remember finding a snail in the turn up of my jeans.

I remember thinking that if I tried hard enough I would be able to distract the TV news reader.

I remember thinking that if an orange had too many pips it wasn't worth eating.

I remember putting a thorn in my brother's friend's football and denying it.

I remember fleecing a drunk at 3 card brag.

I remember how bad I felt when I threw a tennis ball at a dog and hit it in the eye.

I remember running round the sports field fifty times on a stinking hot day for a bet.

I remember Jane Sowden hiding school dinner food, that she wanted to leave, under a lettuce leaf on her plate.

I remember Paul Warburton had really long finger nails and really old parents.

I remember dropping a penny in church and seeing it roll in a big ark and disappear under the font.

I remember Longshore Drift.

I remember my father saying that it is better to own one pair of expensive shoes than ten pairs of cheap ones.

I remember wanting to steal a car.

I remember swinging on the farm gate while my brother went up to the farm house to buy eggs.

I remember when Pete Humphreys played football his blond hair would go dark with sweat except for a bit at the top of his head. It made him look like a coconut.

I remember my father used to stand in the front porch until he heard the Leeds train approach and then sprint up the road to catch it.

I remember setting fire to the community bonfire a week before bonfire night.

I remember seeing the burn scars on Chris Dyson's body in the changing room. He got badly burned dropping a match into the petrol tank of a car.

I remember wondering if a boy at school called Simon Jagger was related to Mick Jagger.

I remember Neil Pollard always getting nose bleeds and having an operation to fix it.

I remember NHS spectacles.

I remember the big crack in our bread board. All the crumbs would get stuck in it.

I remember a market stall in Leeds that had hundreds of 12 inch copies of *The Hollies* 'The air that I breathe'.

I remember being pissed off that the football coach let kids from other villages into our team.

I remember thinking it was odd that the Dutch detective Van Der Valk was played by a British actor.

I remember my mother telling my father he looked like Montgomery Clift.

I remember a receptionist at the doctors having a limp and my mother saying that she won't be able to have children.

I remember my father calling bread rolls scufflers.

I remember Stuart Mason pushing my bag off my desk and breaking my flask.

I remember thinking that David Kirk's older sister looked like a man.

I remember drawing a batman aeroplane.

I remember birds pecking holes in the tops of milk bottles on our step to drink the cream. I thought they were very clever.

I remember the postman was fat and sweaty.

I remember my father betting on a horse called Otter Way to win the Grand National. He went on about it for weeks beforehand. It fell at the first fence.

I remember my friend Tosh telling a girl that her breasts would grow more quickly if she let him feel them. It didn't work.

I remember Kevin Lambert's afro hair.

I remember my Uncle Hans telling me that he spent time in jail in Spain for disrespecting Franco.

I remember hating going to bed when it was still light outside.

I remember drawing an eight point star properly with a compass.

I remember the smell of the bolster on my bed.

I remember sleeping so deeply that the alarm clock didn't wake me.

I *remember* the blue bells at the bully tree woods.

I *remember* Angela Noble kicking her horse and then crying and hugging it.

I *remember* going to a pub with my parents and my father telling me to avoid the bloke at the bar in red trousers as he will certainly be a homosexual.

I *remember* making ginger beer at infants school.

I *remember* my mother telling me that the theme music to 'Manhunt' was Beethoven's 5th Symphony.

I *remember* my shoplifting gang posting my share of a haul through the letter box because I was grounded and couldn't go out.

I *remember* treading in a cow pat and the crispy sound it made.

I *remember* Dr. Wells smoking cigarettes.

I *remember* climbing onto the shed roof and throwing stones at a cat.

I *remember* players getting cramp in the FA Cup final.

I *remember* slices of bread and dripping.

I *remember* the strobe lights at the school disco.

I *remember* 'Rock n Roll Widow' by *Wishbone Ash*.

I remember my sister's future mother-in-law coming to our house and sitting in the car instead of coming in.

I remember my father was always happy when the blossom came out.

I remember wanting to have sex with a black woman.

I remember having all my hair cut off and everyone saying how much better I looked.

I remember thinking that fat people must be lonely.

I remember a gooseberry bush in the garden and it disappearing.

I remember getting depressed on Sunday evenings.

I remember wanting to see inside a prison.

I remember new velvet curtains.

I remember adverts warning of the danger of fireworks.

I remember my mother going to the hairdresser to get her hair set and not knowing what that was.

I remember all our neighbours wanting to shoot the pigeons that were nesting in the rafters and my father saying no and blocking it.

I remember smoking cigarettes at Elland Road waiting for the match to start. The match was on 'Match of the day' and I saw myself on TV smoking. Luckily my father didn't see.

I remember somebody asking me if I was a mod or a rocker.

I remember Mick Ransome not being able to tell the time.

I remember the pleasure of kissing Wendy Jones.

I remember liking a Mary Hopkins song.

I remember skinheads wearing sailor whites and Dr. Marten boots. The really serious ones wore steel toe boots.

I remember my older brother buying meat for his mixed grill every Friday.

I remember Martin Smith had a natural black flash in his brown hair.

I remember camping out in the garden and being so cold I had to come indoors.

I remember hearing that Nigel Wardle had to sleep in swimming trunks because he had so many wet dreams.

I remember Mrs. Varley wearing a coat on a really hot day.

I remember wanting bunk beds.

I remember being teased because my football boots were old fashioned.

I remember selling the winning raffle ticket to a woman in the village. I was taken to her house to deliver a fresh fruit hamper. She was delighted and asked me to choose some fruit for myself. I took a single grape.

I remember wondering why men wear ties (I still do).

I remember putting toilet paper on a comb to make a mouth organ and how blowing on it tickled my lips.

I remember visiting my father in hospital and smuggling in a four pack of beer.

I remember Francis Chichester sailing round the world singlehanded.

I remember doing an English test and answering Alexander Dumas instead of Charles Dickens to the question 'who wrote A Tale of Two Cities?'.

I remember my father hating Harold Wilson.

I remember only once ever heading a football when it didn't hurt.

I remember playing tennis for the first time. It was with a badly warped racket.

I remember my father winning some money on a slot machine and buying us all Knickerbocker Glories.

I remember going to Selby with my parents, my older sister and her boyfriend. They locked me in the car whilst they went drinking.

I remember my sports day mug.

I remember somebody saying in the corner shop that national service should be brought back.

I remember buying a pair of union jack socks.

I remember a weird gardening tool with a half moon head.

I remember my grandad giving my brother his watch.

I remember my father always telling me when he heard the first cuckoo of the year.

I remember how happy I felt when I woke up on holiday to the sound of seagulls.

I remember my sister saying prostitution should be legalised and my father shouting at her.

I remember stealing road signs and storing them behind the garage.

I remember Pot Black.

I remember thinking that Portsmouth and Plymouth were side by side.

I remember hiding my shitty pants at the bottom of the laundry basket.

I remember following a man into the communal toilet in our holiday flat and gagging on the stink he left behind.

I remember the green stagnant water in the maltings pond.

I remember my father buying a sun lamp to ease the pain in his arthritic hip.

I remember building a sand castle and a big kid diving on it.

I remember getting into a special talent group at school for English and not telling my parents.

I remember my parents buying sheepskin rugs from Qualters in Sherburn.

I remember my headmaster Mr. Burnley driving me to Thorne approved school. I had the window down and some paperwork blew out of the window.

I remember my neighbour complaining about the noise my football made when I kicked it against the garage door.

I remember my grandma using my grandad's horseracing form books to line the staircase before a new carpet went down.

I remember my father cooking broad beans in the same pan as a fried egg. The beans set in the egg white and looking at it made me feel weird.

I remember my parents taking Andrew's Liver Salts when they were hungover.

I remember my father never had a decent coat.

I remember going on holiday to Great Yarmouth with Phil Varley's family.

I remember a fire too close to the greenhouse and cracking all the glass.

I remember some big kids dangling me off the air raid shelter.

I remember playing cricket in the school yard and the wickets were two tin boxes.

I remember going to Leeds for the first time and seeing three drunks asleep on a bench propping each other up.

I remember having a 'lawnmower grandad' and not knowing who he was (I still don't).

I remember sherbert dips.

I remember the jug by the bath for rinsing hair.

I remember Gary Sprake throwing the ball into his own net.

I remember hearing my dad say that he loved the Queen. *I remember* thinking how pathetic that was.

I remember getting stomach ache because my school trousers were too tight.

I remember the funeral scene in 'Callan'.

I remember empty bottles of Magnet Pale Ale on the scullery floor.

I remember corned beef fritters in school dinners.

I remember calling on my friend. His mother answered the door in bare feet and I thought she must have just had sex. It made me feel really awkward.

I remember the landlord at the Black Bull pub wore a wig.

I remember the Dickens collection on the piano.

I remember my mother saying that Auntie Mary was a snob because she lived in Potters Bar.

I remember hating that my younger sister was at my school.

I remember somebody built a wonky wall outside the post office. It wasn't quirky just really badly built.

I remember Motown Chartbusters records.

I remember dreading the first day of every new term because the teacher always read out full names and I would get laughed at.

I remember Neville Shute books.

I remember my older brother getting a big parcel of stuff about Mao Tse Tung.

I remember the first time I smoked weed.

I remember watching 'The World at War' and sneaking off to cry about the jews in the concentration camps.

I remember wondering where shit goes.

I remember putting red cardinal stain on the corner of the back step.

I remember going to the playing field with my little brother and his new football on Christmas morning. The ball bounced into the road and got hit by a car. It was all out of shape and we both tried not to cry.

I remember that once during an argument my mother tried to pour a pot of hot tea over my father.

I remember we had a milk churn that we used to catch the water from the washing machine to water the garden in draughts.

I remember my little brother falling down the back steps. He landed on a milk bottle and gashed his nose really bad.

I remember my father lifting up the fattest man in the village for a bet.

I remember thinking that my mother was in dispute with the whole world.

I remember my father singing 'The Puppet' by Tom Jones. I sang it after him because I thought it would make him happy but he didn't seem to notice.

I remember my grandma cooking me egg on toast.

I remember thinking Ottoman was an odd word.

I remember play fighting with my father and breaking his false teeth.

I remember somebody in the village coming home on leave from the navy and telling us that he went to the Ali-Frazier fight.

I remember Rod Spalton drinking at our house one Christmas and getting so drunk he drove his yellow three wheeler van over our garden.

I remember the people three doors up fostered two black boys and their dad used to visit every Saturday.

I remember Tosh's stepmother was always drinking coke and his Father chain smoking JPS cigarettes.

I remember my headmaster using his assembly speech to condemn Mick Jagger's appearance on the previous evening's Top of the Pops.

I remember my father telling me he liked the look of Emma Peel in the Avengers. It was the one and only time he said anything remotely sexual to me.

I remember a Rod Argent record.

I remember hitting the stamp machine outside the post office with my toy rifle. It spewed out stamps and I panicked and stuffed them down a grate.

I remember Mandy Zahler's father taking her to the swings and secretly swigging from a half bottle of whiskey.

I remember my grandad's weekly treat was a bag of monkey nuts from Pontefract market.

I remember Zetters pools coupons.

I remember putting brilliant white laces into filthy trainers.

I remember my mother saying that my trainers smelled like rotten vegetables.

I remember the washing machine breaking down and my father using one with a mangle.

I remember dreading my little brother waking up as he would always cry and put my mother in a bad mood.

I remember Stuart Stabler punching Peter Robinson so hard that his teeth went through his lip. There was a shocking amount of blood. He ran to his sister's house for tissues.

I remember earning £2 a day picking potatoes.

I remember Brutus jeans with embroided high waste bands.

I remember going to the York City v Manchester United match and nobody believing that I had gone.

I remember Bert Wardle's raincoat as he walked home past our house every evening.

I remember the brightly coloured art deco shot glasses in the left hand side of the bar in the front room.

I remember half pint glasses that had contained shampoo at Christmas.

I remember not knowing what bootleg records were.

I remember Mr. Burnley's gold tooth.

I remember fighting with a boy three years older than me. I got two black eyes and told my parents I had been hit by snowballs.

I *remember* seeing a dead mouse in a mouse trap.

I *remember* reading 'The Cruel Sea' to impress my father but he didn't notice.

I *remember* the Double Deckers TV show on a Saturday morning.

I *remember* my father sharpening the carving knife. The noise set my teeth on edge.

I *remember* my father cancelling the Yorkshire Evening Post. He said we didn't need two papers a day.

I *remember* the Gambols cartoon in the *Daily Express*.

I *remember* my father's pipe and St. Bruno tobacco.

I *remember* the cigar in my father's top draw. It belonged to my grandad.

I *remember* how the hairbrush in the kitchen drawer always seemed to be tangled in a load of string.

I *remember* the 'Never Mind' statue on the landing window sill. It was chipped.

I *remember* polishing the lino floors and buffing them by putting rags on my feet and sliding around.

I *remember* the horsewhip on the top shelf of the kitchen cupboard.

I remember the squeaky sound that the clothes rack made when it was pulled up.

I remember my older brother buying his own milk. He was so worried that we would drink it that he hid it and it went sour.

I remember the pattern on the wallpaper that was used to line the drawers in my bedroom.

I remember the new doctor's surgery opening next door to us.

I remember my little brother asking me for a drag of my cigarette. I turned it round just as he was about to put it in his mouth and it burned his lips really badly. I still feel bad about this.

I remember wondering why my older brother was way more posh than the rest of us.

I remember my father's slippers.

I remember thinking that the new teacher's skirt was too short.

I remember going to Terry's chocolate factory in Reg Harker's lorry.

I remember a sugar shortage.

I remember the shop keeper's son slicing cheese with really dirty hands.

I remember how my grandma's poodle always nipped my feet when I tried to leave the room.

I remember a boy at school couldn't run without humming really loudly. We beat him up to make him stop but it didn't work.

I remember one drought summer a farmer redirected the beck to irrigate his fields. It ran dry and we poked around in the mud.

I remember always poking out my tongue when I concentrated.

I remember sheltering from the rain in the Harley's passage.

I remember feeling sad when I looked at ploughed fields.

I remember smashing a school thermometer to get the mercury.

I remember pretending to go to the toilet in the football changing rooms so nobody saw the holes in my socks.

I remember how cool I thought it was that Andrew Laycock was sent home to put his school uniform on and he returned on a combine harvester.

I remember Wensleydale cheese and beetroot sandwiches.

I remember Mr. Hick had a bad twitch.

I remember seeing Eric Clapton with my sister in Scarborough.

I remember seeing a dog called Brandy kill a rat.

I remember playing cricket in the school yard and how you always got extra runs if the ball went into the boy's toilet.

I remember Leeds United being called 'Bridesmaids' and not understanding what it meant.

I remember my teacher putting a map of Great Britain on the wall and asking who knew where 'The Wash' was.

I remember being confused that Cassius Clay changed his name to Muhammed Ali.

I remember finding it impossible to cut bread straight (I still can't).

I remember winning a medal at a cricket tournament and Stuart Stabler grabbing it and throwing it away. He was on the losing side in the final.

I remember hearing that you should never wear a suit jacket separate from the tousers.

I remember going into hospital for a long time. A girl asked me why I was in there. I didn't know as no one had told me. I had pneumonia and nearly died.

I remember my mother putting a long deep scratch in the welsh dresser with a half crown coin after a violent argument with my father.

I remember hiding in the house for hours and wondering why nobody was looking for me.

I remember snapping sprouts off their stalks on a frosty morning in my father's garden.

I remember seeing the lice in Jamie Bielby's hair.

I remember drinking neat vinegar from the jars of pickled eggs at Christmas.

I remember the bottles of milk being put on the radiators at school to warm them up. We all wanted to drink the milk cold.

I remember sneaking into my mother's bedroom and wiping dog shit on her dresses because I felt such anger and hatred towards her.

I remember making a bird's nest from lawn trimmings and my father putting an egg in it and pretending it had been laid by a hen.

I remember adopting a stray dog and an old woman accosting me in the butcher's shop accusing me of stealing it from her.

I remember finding my father asleep in the bath and it was so cold that ice had formed on the bath water.

I remember my older sister's first day at work. She was fourteen and was starting as a trainee hairdresser in the Marshall and Snellgrove department store in Leeds.

I remember great uncle Tom visiting from Barrow in Furness. It happened to be my birthday and he gave me a ten shilling note. It was the most money I had ever had and the happiest I had ever felt. My father borrowed that money from me and I never saw it again.

I remember my mother falling over on the wet scullery floor. She knocked herself out and me and my sister danced with happiness because we thought she was dead.

I remember kids in my village thinking that my older brother was gay.

I remember trying to split a golf ball with an axe. The head flew off and gashed my head (I've still got the scar).

I remember collecting old lemonade bottles and returning them to the shop for the halfpenny deposit. I bought fish and chips with the money.

I remember a man in the village giving me an old army drinking bottle. I never drank from it because my mother said it was dirty.

I remember going outside for the first time after recovering from pneumonia.

I remember being ashamed of my shoes.

I remember thinking that the council estate in my village was Coronation Street.

I remember the recreation ground flooding and trying to swim in the flood water.

I remember being terrified of wood lice as I thought they were like German soldiers.

I remember seeing Tim Rawlinson for the first time in glasses. I felt a stab of pain because I knew he would be bullied.

I remember seeing a dying baby bird. Steven Marshall put it out of its misery because I couldn't do it.

I remember the fear I felt for Hilary Blackburn. She once made me hit a dog with a stick.

I remember seeing a child hit on the head by a swing and feeling amazed that he didn't cry.

I remember eating tripe with my grandad.

I remember Mick Ransome's mother dying. He stopped brushing his teeth.

I remember my mother, in the middle of an argument with my father, telling him that his father comes round hassling her for sex.

I remember knocking the plaster off the wall in the front room as a result of banging my head on the armchair.

I remember Boo Jenkinson blowing up a frog with a straw.

I remember seeing the corpse of a dog floating in the maltings pond.

I remember a whole batch of double yoke eggs.

I remember wanting to be a heroin addict.

I remember lying about my whereabouts and going to London to see *'Bad Company'*.

I remember breaking into the youth club to steal the subs money.

I remember my school burning down and people thinking that I did it.

I remember being terrified of the cockerel in Graham Hill's henhouse.

I remember Boo Jenkinson pissing down the slide at the playground. He was shamed in the school assembly.

I remember running away with a tent and getting as far as Scotch Corner before the police brought me back.

I remember being caught stealing sweets from the corner shop. I felt such shame that I went home to bed and pretended to be sick.

I remember throwing up just as extra time started during the England v West Germany World Cup quarter final in 1970.

I remember thinking that my older brother was so favoured by my parents that he was really Prince Charles.

I remember stealing a sack full of Christmas cards from the post office sorting office as I figured that some of the cards would have cash in them (I was right).

I remember stealing two books of raffle tickets from the football club and selling them and keeping the money.

I remember my father burning buckets full of used sanitary towels.

I remember going to a harvest festival on my own and taking a tin of sliced peaches.

I remember collecting PG Tips football cards.

I remember Gary Lunt drowning in the bacon factory pond.

I remember throwing stones into the darkness and running when I hit the greenhouses.

I remember the Queen driving very slowly through our village.

I remember waiting all day to see the *'Flying Scotsman'* pass through Gascoigne Wood junction.

I remember wanting to have sex with 'Cat Woman'.

I remember my father packing his suitcase to leave home after a row with my mother. He placed his electric razor in the bottom right hand corner of his case.

I remember coming downstairs late one night because I had wet the bed. I found my father asleep in the chair drunk and my mother on the floor with uncle Jim. He had his hand up her skirt.

I remember wanting to kill my mother because she sent me to bed and I missed the moon landing.

I remember sneaking round the back of the Women's Institute and seeing people playing in a beetle drive.

I remember wondering why my father never protected me from my mother.

I remember somebody at school telling me my mother was a shagbag.

I remember my father once listened to an entire classical music record on the wrong speed.

I remember playing 'Mite' in the village pantomime.

I remember the label on the Camp coffee bottle.

I remember my sister buying the record 'Lily the Pink' with her first wage.

I remember shaving the bark off the holly bush in our garden with a razor blade.

I remember gypsies coming to our door to sell clothes pegs.

I remember the black face of the coal delivery man Mr. Batey.

I remember going swimming at Selby baths and afterwards buying broken biscuits from Woolworths.

I remember cutting a hole in my paper round sack so I could slip my hand through it to steal sweets at the shop.

I remember my brother's two best friends dying in a motorbike crash in Amsterdam.

I remember my mother knitting me an orange polo neck sweater. It hurt to pull it over my head and she ran out of wool so the right shoulder was a slightly different colour. I wore it once to Gary Rawlinson's birthday party and everyone laughed at me.

I remember hating *The Black And White Minstrel Show*.

I remember weighing up whether or not my life would be better if I was in borstal.

I remember overhearing a neighbour calling me 'droopy drawers'.

I remember going on a school trip to Harewood House and climbing into the wishing well to steal the money.

I remember my sister thinking that the saying 'As far as the eye can see' meant the 'Ican' sea was an actual place.

I remember Billy Hunter's ice cream van and that the ice cream had tiny bits of ice in it.

I remember finding out that Neil Pollard got free school dinners and him begging me not to tell anyone.

I remember sending off Quaker Oats vouchers to get a free football. When it arrived I was upset that it wasn't as good as my friend's Wembley Trophy football.

I remember Nicholas Holt making me kiss a stone that he had just pissed on.

I remember being terrified watching 'Whatever Happened to Baby Jane'.

I remember having bananas and Blue Riband wafers as a Friday night treat when my mother was in a good mood.

I remember having to wear plastic sandals from Woolworths. Only poor kids wore them.

I remember looking over my father's shoulder when he was doing the crossword and how amazed he was when I knew that the answer to 1 across was 'absconded'.

I remember getting paid 12 shillings and sixpence a week for doing two paper rounds six days a week.

I remember when decimalisation was introduced that my wages became sixty two and a half pence.

I remember picking peas in the school holidays and being scared of the rough women.

I remember firing a cap gun into my father's eye when he was sleeping in the arm chair (If he had caught me that day I'd still have the scars).

I remember seeing my older sister in sunglasses and thinking she looked like a blind person.

I remember 'The Laughing Cavalier' picture on the kitchen wall.

I remember the smell of the old car in our garage.

I remember a wooden club type thing that you put socks on to darn them.

I remember calling currant squares 'fly pie'.

I remember a Green Gage plum tree.

I remember purple heather on the North Yorkshire moors.

I remember the doctor's son next door had a toy car he could sit in.

I remember my mother saying that my sister's stubbornness was a good thing.

I remember feeling like I was always walking up really steep hills.

I remember wearing a new pair of Levis in the bath to shrink them.

I remember sitting in the waiting room at Leeds train station wearing my army surplus great coat. I had my eyes closed and a policeman approached my because he thought I was a vagrant. I was delighted as this was exactly the look I was cultivating.

I remember feeling that my life had changed after watching the *Led Zeppelin* film 'The Song Remains the Same'.

I remember envying kids who didn't have middle names.

I remember my first migraine and thinking I was
   going blind.

I remember Tangerine Dream playing in York Minster.

I remember setting up a car cleaning round.

I remember my older brother going to university and
   thinking he was mad for coming home every
   weekend.

I remember feeling closer to my sister Fiona than my
   other siblings.

I remember crow's nests in the trees near the railway.

I remember my father using 'ladies man' as a
   derogatory term.

I remember Geoff Thornton's mother giving me a box
   of hot dogs to carry to the village bonfire. I ate five
   of them on the way.

I remember a one eyed doll.

I remember my older brother being put on a pedestal
   because of his qualifications. When I got older I
   realised that in reality they were deeply
   unimpressive and I am far more qualified than him.

I remember 'never cast a clout until May is out'.

I remember really wanting to do something (like join
   the choir) and then really not wanting to do it.

I remember   Andy Robinson's big ears.

I remember   the man who ran the post office had a big pile of manure right outside his back door.

I remember   Lucy Grice's mother had a chitty chitty bang bang car.

I remember   jokes on ice cream sticks.

I remember   my older brother's first girlfriend was called Carmel.

I remember   the village notice board always had the cricket team pinned on it.

I remember   Dave Hill's nicotine stained fingers.

I remember   my sister falling off her platform shoes.

I remember   seeing a tramp for the first time. I told my teacher and he said the term 'gentleman of the road' was better than tramp.

I remember   wondering why my younger siblings were so blonde.

I remember   Richard Green was Robin Hood.

I remember   Johnny Weismuller was Tarzan.

I remember   Robinson Crusoe.

I remember   the American bicentenary celebrations.

I remember thinking that dirty things happened in Soho.

I remember picking gunshot pellets out of a rabbit stew.

I remember photographs stuffed inside the smoking cabinet.

I remember 'High Noon'

I remember Bero self raising flour.

I remember a couple having sex in the long grass near Steeton Hall.

I remember a big pile of burning tyres and how the smoke tasted in the back of my throat.

I remember my parents calling turds 'Jumbos'.

I remember starting the 'Tony Currie for England' in the kop at Elland Road.

I remember big blocks of lard piled on top of each other in the larder.

I remember a cattle stampede in a cowboy film.

I remember trying to steal a pile of national saving stamps from the post office by distracting the cashier. I failed.

I remember my parents talking about the Hanratty case.

I remember Watergate and not understanding it.

I remember the Spassky v Fischer chess match.

I remember a controversy about a rude joke on 'Jokers Wild'.

I remember always feeling sad when I was cruel to another kid.

I remember Christian Barnard and the first open heart surgery.

I remember the smell of rape seed and thinking it smelt like my mother when she had just got out of bed.

I remember a cricket ball smashing through a wooden seed box.

I remember thinking that I dread too many things.

I remember a pot of bitumen catching fire.

I remember feeling like I was the only one who knew my father was a weak man.

I remember standing in front of a railway signal and refusing to move until it went up.

I remember the controversy about PJ Proby splitting his pants on stage.

I remember hitting a cricket ball into the long grass. It took me ages to find it and when I did all my mates sang the Cliff Richard song 'Congratulations'.

I remember thinking the Beadnell family were weirdly sexual and promiscuous.

I remember my father saying the miners were holding the country to ransom

I remember sniffing spent fireworks.

I remember day dreaming that when I left home I would never go back.

I remember a pal, Richard Earless, saying that in the future women won't need to have sex with men to get pregnant (how prescient!).

I remember trying to work out how big the ark was in the bible to take all those huge animals.

I remember knowing that my mouth always got me into trouble but not caring.

I remember planning to roll a drunk but my partner in crime wouldn't do it.

I remember the first Asian presenter of 'Look North'.

I remember hearing that Elvis Presley was going to appear at Batley Variety Club. He didn't.

I remember having to try really hard not to set fire to stuff.

I remember that the World at War coming on TV on Sunday just as it got dark was my version of hell.

I remember always feeling more street wise than my older siblings.

I remember Andy Stewart singing in a kilt.

I remember my father was always rude about the Irish.

I remember thinking that the Great Train robbers were the coolest men on earth.

9 781789 630671